MW00935993

Heartscapes

Meryl Ann Olson

authorHOUSE®

AuthorHouse™
1663 Liberty Drive
Bloomington, IN 47403
www.authorhouse.com
Phone: 1 (800) 839-8640

© 2015 Meryl Ann Olson. All rights reserved.

No part of this book may be reproduced, stored in
a retrieval system, or transmitted by any means
without the written permission of the author.

Published by AuthorHouse 09/12/2016

ISBN: 978-1-5049-6223-0 (sc)
ISBN: 978-1-5049-6222-3 (e)

Print information available on the last page.

Any people depicted in stock imagery provided by Thinkstock are
models, and such images are being used for illustrative purposes only.
Certain stock imagery © Thinkstock.

This book is printed on acid-free paper.

Because of the dynamic nature of the Internet, any web
addresses or links contained in this book may have changed
since publication and may no longer be valid. The views
expressed in this work are solely those of the author and do
not necessarily reflect the views of the publisher, and the
publisher hereby disclaims any responsibility for them.

Table of Contents

I dedicate this first anthology of poetry to my precious Mom, Arleen, who encouraged me to write, send out my poems for publication, and hopefully, to be able to share my pain, joy, hope, faith, and love for Self, God, and all beings. May everyone everywhere be touched by God's infinite grace.

Thanks to my beau, Gary, who helped me edit, self publish, and get all these poems into a beautiful form.

I dedicate all these poems to my Lord, Jesus, the Christ, and Goddess Gaia, our precious Mother Earth, who gives me hope every day. Both Father God & Divine Mother inspire me with wonder, joy, and awe at the beauty within and all around me.

Foreword

You are about to read "Heartscapes", a collection of poems written over a period of 40 years.

During this period, I found my spiritual teacher, Swami Muktananda, an Indian guru (who called me Niranjani). I was married and divorced twice, gave birth naturally to three children without medication, attempted suicide multiple times, was diagnosed with bipolar disorder (manic depression), and miraculously, through the grace of God and love of family and friends, was able to survive all my trials to come to a place of peace, unconditional love, and acceptance. I see my entire path as a great blessing to myself and others. My poems in chronological order reflect all the ups and downs of the illness and cover a variety of topics from lost love, my love of God within and without, to nature and sacred sex. Some are musings and prayers to Great Spirit. Writing poetry helps me understand myself better and gives me an outlet for my deepest feelings, secrets, and reflections on life.

The story of my life is recorded in "By Grace I Dance – How I Survived Suicide, Manic Depression and Marriage", to be published in 2016.

Poems

The Love I Miss (Oct 1976)

Where did it all go?
The love that once was ours
The times I said I loved you so, the times you brought
    me flowers
The gentleness in word and touch has somehow gone
    astray
How could that sweetness change so much
Just living day to day
You say black, I say white
We've changed so much I fear
Now as different as day and night
When once so close, so dear
There's no legal commitment, ties should be easy to
    break
You probably want OUT too
Shouldn't be tough to undertake
But who wants the cats
Who gets the TVs ….
I think that's probably the least of our worries
For with all our problems I still love you so
And I would give you the earth's gems if you let me
    know that you feel the same
Let's stop this silly game and start anew
It can't be that difficult to do

Tell me what's wrong
I'll change if I can
It's to you I want to belong
It's YOU I want to be my man
Give me back the days when you lovingly brushed my
    long hair
And we talked all night until the dawn brought a
    beautiful new day
And we laughed without a care
If we can't then please let it die
You don't see, but alone I cry
Your tenderness, your love I miss
But fear not, if you go I'll get by

~/~

Listen (Nov 1976)

Two? Four?? Six?!! Eight???!!!
Hours you sit and stagnate in front of the box they call
    for boobs
Soon your brain will become one with wires, screen,
    and tubes
Is it too late not to reap what "they" have sewn?
Or can you still differentiate which thoughts are
    "theirs" and which your own
If not the tube to amuse yourself there's always the
    disc
Can silence be so painful
To listen such a risk

To create a thought that comes from within instead of
without
creates no sin without a doubt
A novel, a lyric, maybe a script
A greeting card sent to a friend who is sick
All these are creative
Past idleness condoned
What a feeling of pride to know these are your own
Or do you even dare to become completely still?
Of your mind's endless wanderings have you had your
fill
Are you ready to take a smoother course
Ready to receive from a higher Source
A few silent moments with your God Self each day
Might find a treasure lost
Prevent a holocaust
Or just help ease your way
So next time you want to turn on the TV or listen to
the DJ set your mind free for just a few moments
To see what the small voice within has to say
Some guidance, inspiration
All this will come to you
If only you will take some time to renew and
LISTEN

Meryl Ann Olson

The Key (Nov 1980)

for D.H.

You, you've changed my life
You, you and your way
I feel so happy inside that I could cry
How I love you

You're like sunshine caressing my face
When I'm with you or just by myself
I can feel your lasting embrace
How I love you

For the first time in my life I feel balanced and alive
I need everyone—I need no one
I'm a part of God's Whole
We're all One—Yes we are, yes we are
I want to give all myself to you, Lord, and mankind
I had been so fragmented
Hiding from my self
but now I find that the power of Love's within me
and you've helped me to find the Key
to unlock the gateway to my heart

Chorus
I have a lock and you hold the Key
When I think of all the love inside
God sets my spirit free
when I remember Thee is Me

~/~

The Willow (July 1981)

Oh perfect Willow
Your splendid pulchritude
is imbedded in my consciousness
So tall and strong
Commanding and majestic
Yet with a softness and feminine loveliness
that brings me to wonder and tears
Each time I am in your holy presence
Is it the breeze that accents your beauty
Or you who adorn it with your flowing tresses

Teach me to be like you
    CENTERED
And firmly grounded to the earth
But always willing to bend and dance with the wind
Your arms Outstretched R e A C H I N G
TOUCHING
The wonders of the world
KNOWING
That all is perfection
As You Are

~/~

Meryl Ann Olson

By Your Grace (May 1982)

Verse

One day in my inner temple I prayed for a teacher to
    guide me
You heard the language of my heart, you saw what
    was inside me
You said that I had earned your love and you would
    never leave me
and when I faltered on my path you lovingly
    retrieved me

Chorus

By your grace I can see past darkness into light
By your grace I am free to reach the highest height
By your grace I now know who I truly am
By your grace your sweet grace I am free

2nd Verse

The lesson of attachment is a painful one to learn
I was bound by the past-there seemed nowhere to turn
I thought somehow I'd lost you when everything went
    wrong
But you were with me all the time to help me become
    strong

Chorus

3rd Verse

When I had my fill of suffering I decided to let go
I then surrendered to Your Will and quickly came to
      know
That all had gone just as we'd planned-the pain helped
      me to grow
And now I think I understand that place from where
      love flows

Chorus

4th Verse

I finally met you face to face and in that timeless hour
You brought me to that special place
My heart bloomed like a flower
I felt enveloped in your love-I knew I was divine
I'm free and peaceful like a dove
All the world is mine!

Chorus

By your grace, your sweet grace I am free!

Words & Music Meryl Niranjani

Meryl Ann Olson

Little One (April 1984)

Little one my little one
Now your life has just begun
Will it be what I hope for you?
Will you find the sadguru?
Life is short—just a grain of sand
passing through the hourglass
Will you trust? Will you hold his hand
On your way as life doth pass
Travel far if you must roam
til you find your heart's your home
Journey 'til your search is through
When you've found the Lord's in you

Now my simple song is done
Making rhymes is a lot of fun
Hope you're happy your whole life through
Entrust it to the God in you

Meryl Ann Olson

Lost and Found Again (Nov 1987)

**penned at Siddha Meditation ashram in South
    Fallsburg, NY**

I got lost again
in the maze of my mind
But this time I left my good sense behind
I thought that putting a bullet in my brain
would take away the fear and stop the pain
How tragic, how insane!
If only I could set my soul free from my body
I'd be at peace again
I'd live in ecstasy
If only I could have stopped all the dark thoughts
I could have quieted my mind to go inside
To that place of perfect stillness
Where love and peace reside
But this was not meant to be my destiny
I could have been lost for a very long time
Never to be with my sweet family again
Never to reason or rhyme
But your Grace saved me again
Through your miracles I'm almost back to new
How can I thank you
What can I do
To show my gratitude for a second chance at life
In this body without the pain and strife
In this beautiful temple you gave me
This place where God resides

It was only the power of Love that could save me
My Lord's and my own Love that always guides
Me through each trial and tribulation
I've been through in my time
The love that is so precious
so blissful, so sublime
I could never be apart from that Love
No matter what my mind thinks
Is a drop ever separate from the Ocean
Even when a ship sinks

Meryl Niranjani Olson

Illusions (Aug 1991)

I thought you were my dream man
My knight in shining armor
A man of tenderness and devotion
Who had a desire to know God
A spiritual man of beauty and vision
Who could devote his life to me and my dreams
But, alas, 'twas all an illusion
In a moment's time I thought I knew you
We thought we were meant for each other for eternity
But we were blinded by our passion
By an inner feeling of love that seemed inexplicable
Now we know better, I think.

Only a selfish, lonely man does not love and
    appreciate children
Their bright lights and magical smiles
'Tis a joyless person who does not desire to become a
    vessel
To become a guardian to watch over God's perfect
    souls
God's little angels
Bearing them and guiding them to know the Self
To experience the majesty and wisdom of the Lord's
    perfect
Universe within and all around themselves.
There's so much I cannot share with you
Suddenly you seem shallow and empty to me
You have nothing to offer me
How could you expect me to leave my dear ones
For a lonely life with you
They are my precious beloveds
Hearts of my heart, Lights of my life
They're not perfect, I know.
But I still dream Ari and Kyri will be with me again
    someday
And live with me and my mate in harmony and bliss
How would you think I would give up a sweet life like
    this?
For a man who has nothing
For a man who loves no one but his own self.
I think I'll put this dream back on the shelf.
You were just an illusion

And I am that elusive butterfly you once dreamed
    about
But weren't daring enough to fully know, to fully
    pursue
Maybe we'll meet again in another life
One that's not filled with illusions.

~/~

Eating to Fill Their Soul's Longing (Sept 1995)

All over America from Kalamazoo to the Big Apple
I see women eating to fill their soul's longing
They gorge on popcorn, potato chips, pizza, and beer
in front of the boob tube watching soaps and reruns of
A Star is Born with Judy Garland waiting to be
    discovered
As we hear her happily belt out "The Man That Got
    Away"
We long to fill up the emptiness in our guts
That's so deep it bores a hole straight through to our
    ovaries
The time long gone when we believed our Prince
    Charming would come
The princeful fantasy turning out to be a real toad of
    a tale
A fable that taught us to look outside ourselves to find
    our dream

The pot of gold at the end of a spiraling double
      rainbow
The evanescent light of our souls

Countless knights in shining armor down the road
They gorge on junk food to fill up the emptiness
      inside
While I become thinner and thinner
Going to bed hungry with a vibrator and a bottle of
      sangria
To quench the emotional thirst and
Drown out the cries of my soul

Now I retch at the thought of them
Those false gladiators in their tarnished armor
Their broken promises no longer piercing the shield
I've built around my heart
Some of us erect huge fortresses of fat fueled by rage
      and longing
As for me I am sick to death of my self-made prison
I'm famished for the Truth of my Being
I pray to the Goddess beseeching Her
Divine Mother please fulfill my soul's craving with
      the nectar of Divine Love
I can now toss these mortal decaying suitors aside
Into the flames of Kali's kitchen fire
And marry my own inner flame
Finally having drunk from the Lord's chalice
I revel in pure delight

Blissfully drunk on the true wine
That quenches my lifelong hunger and thirst

Meryl

~/~

Divorced (June 1996)

penned at IWWG conference in Saratoga Springs

Don't lose your shirt in the divorce like I lost mine
Sunken bare chest exposing breaking heart
One that still felt so much a part of you, our children,
     and our happy home
Our seemingly perfect little life in our big new
     country house
And our happy ever after love I never thought would die….
     Until I made the fatal mistake one full moon
     night in June
Of trying to blow my brains out in our bedroom
You were out for the night with Ariel, our son, my
     little bear, my beloved one
Whom I carried and birthed at home in blissful
     intimacy with you
Then held and suckled for two years at my
     overflowing happy breasts
How could I leave him with you now?
He is mine, too, you see

I gave him life, he's in my blood, he is a part of Me
He was three and she was toddling, my precious Kyrieh
Barely got to know her it seemed before the madness
      took me away
My slick lady lawyer said I could keep them if I
      wanted
In our peaceful and "equitable" distribution
During divorce negotiations you took me aside and
      made me see the light
You were the stronger more stable one
You were so convincing I didn't put up a fight
I saw no choice but to give you the kids and the house
      that shelters them too
Besides I could never afford the mortgage you told me
Seemed there was not much I could do
"Remember you're handicapped", you said
"And, you don't have a job"
But you could have supported us for a while
you arrogant anal retentive snob!
Eight years have passed, the pain has subsided
I've made a life of my own, my self confidence
      has grown
Time to be happy and free, I've decided
Great Spirit guided me to go back to school while
      raising my second baby girl
The long road is almost done
A Bachelor's degree will soon be mine and life has
      just begun
The man I see loves me as I am and I'm feeling fine

Our time together a sacred respite from the busy life
    I lead
Our loving so divine, our sexy spirits freed
Who'd have thought after all that pain and loss Great
    Spirit would provide all the love I need

Meryl

Tantra The Lover out of Boundless Love has Become My Beloved (July 1996)

**penned at Skidmore College during IWWG
    "Remember the Magic"**

I am lost in your intimate embrace
Impaled upon your pulsating Wand of Light
Your tanned muscular arms and hands supporting
My nude petite form from underneath
My silky smooth round bottom
Bare perky creamy white breasts with large erect pink
    nipples
Engulfed by your white haired open- hearted chest
Beating hearts and pelvises joined as One
Our lips and Souls connected for life
The warm sun caresses my face
as a kind gentle breeze wafts through the tops

Of the sweet green sycamore trees
Cooling me, loving me
I gaze deeply into your clear blue eyes
Pure as rain
As you lift me up and down
Then slowly rock me back and forth in a steady
    rhythm
For what could be hours
Or maybe it's minutes I don't know
I have gone to a place where there is no time
I can only Be in Ecstasy
Transported to a celestial realm
Where there is only sublime peace, bliss, and love
I close my radiant golden eyes
And melt into a still place deep within myself
Simultaneously melting into you
No boundaries whatsoever
After a while the I that once was me ceases to be
She has merged with the Great Ocean of Life itself
And I AM One with the Beloved I once believed
Existed outside of me
Now nothing exists but the Goddess
And I've become my own sweet cherished Beloved

Rev. Meryl Niranjani

Meryl Ann Olson

A Place Beyond (April 1998)

There is a place beyond sound
Within sound
Where there is no sound
In the middle of the forest
Amidst the cacophony of the chirping crickets
Buzzing cicadas, croaking frogs
Bird calls, and other animal chatter is the sound of
      nothingness
Beyond the primordial impulse of Aum
Was and is perfect stillness
The VOID
Where I can refresh myself and experience
Sublime inner peace
Come, my children
Walk into my forest
And hug a tree
She will completely love and refresh thee

Meryl Niranjani

Fabulous Form (May 1999)

for Ariel, my Firstborn
Out of nothing, pure BEING
Came the Everything
In one abrupt explosion

A pulsation, A bursting forth
Of the One into the many
A tiny cell divides and multiplies into
A living, breathing creature
Infinitesimal forms
Fifteen years ago today I, Woman Goddess
Birthed pure consciousness
A being of infinite intelligence who'd been forming
    inside
My warm loving womb for nine miraculous months
Fashioning itself into matching arms and legs, head,
    heart organs, and, brain
Ten tiny fingers and toes
Bright blue eyes turned hazel like moms after six
    months
I still vividly recall that first precious moment at
    10:31 AM
After a full day and night of loving labor at home
On my knees upon our bed
Putting my hand down by my warm vagina
Soaring higher than a free floating kite
Feeling your baby head hanging there
My mind in disbelief
My body felt relief
You were so soft and wet
In satisfied exhaustion I finally lay back after twelve
    hours
Letting the midwives complete your delivery
When you were finally free of my womb you cried
But when they lay your beautiful body

Upon my chest you felt comforted
And I was in Heaven
Though your head was cone shaped and
The rest of you yellow with jaundice you were
The most beautiful baby I'd ever seen
My little boy smelled so sweet
Your skin so soft it nearly melted into mine
We gazed into each others' eyes
As if we had always been together
My beloved Ariel, my son
Light of my life, my precious one
Happy birthday, my beloved
I am so grateful you are in my sweet life

I Am a Delicious Apple Tree (June 1999)

I am here to serve you

Please notice me
Allow my beauty and grace
To awaken and refresh your divine spirit

Nourish your weary soul
Please don't be afraid of me
I am your Sister

Come sit beside me
Come hug me
Wrap your tired arms around me

Feel the strength and energy
Running through my vibrant body

Feel my peace

Hear my ancient wisdom
The stories of our ancestors
Are buried deep within my bark
And travel all the way down to my roots
The stories of our Divine Mother

Eons and ages go by
I never change
I just stand here Being the Witness to all the stories
of your lives
Loving the breeze as it tickles my leafy branches
Come take time to Know Me

I am here to serve you
And the Great Ones, Glorious Beings
of Light
Beautiful brothers and sisters

Please partake of my wisdom and my fruit

Climb up my smooth body and crawl

Into my branches, dear Children
Partake of my sweet fruit
Then jump off and fall laughingly into
Fluffy green grass below my billowing branches

Meryl A. Olson

~/~

If Only (Oct 1999)

If only I could be gentler with myself
If only I could shower myself with all the love and
        affection I give to others
If only I didn't need others approval to feel whole
If only I could praise myself for being the best I know
        how to be in each moment
If only I were not so hard on myself
If only I hadn't hurt myself
If only I were not so needy
If only I could be happy with myself and need nothing
        from outside to feel complete
If onlys will get me nothing and nowhere
Please help me, Lord, to accept myself as I am.

~/~

I Am the Willow (Nov 1999)

I Am the Willow
Bowing her head low
To Father Sky blue Lord
Celestial sun showering golden
Radiant beams upon my flowing tresses
Of gay green Love Light

I am firmly grounded through my beaming brown
     trunk to Mother
Stretching out chunky roots to the core crystal of Gaia

While my arms of Light raise up high into the
     azure sky
Of stars and moons and Gods in highest praise
I sing and sway with the wind
As it dances through my wispy tresses of gold and
     green
I am flexible and rooted
I am pure unencumbered Joy
A tribute to the Magnificent One
I Am Meryl the Infinite Sacred Priestess of Love

Mother of God and the Universe
Once I offered my head to a bullet
As I said OM Namah Shivaya, sacred mantra of
     protection
Many cried for me
I cried for myself
So many years of suffering
Of not feeling Whole
Now the ego is annihilated
There is only Love and Bliss
Only the gentle Beauty that I Am
There is only sweet sublime Peace
Since I offered everything up to the Great One
I am His alone
I am so blessed and utterly grateful

My body belongs to Goddess Gaia
But my heart belongs to Shiva, my Divine Husband
Pure as jasmine, more radiant than a million suns
We have merged again, my precious Beloved
And I am Yours through eternity
I am now the Eternal Witness of this Divine Play of
     Ours my Lord
Let me praise you with every breath, word, action,
     and thought
I am Thine

Rev. Meryl Niranjani

~/~

Kyrie: Our First Years Together (April 2000)

She was born on a sunny day
My beautiful daughter Kyrieh
She was a little late
Sunday we went to the ashram for a blessing
For our new bundle of joy we could not wait
I awoke after a night of sweet dreams
On that auspicious Monday morn
Who'd have guessed after six short hours of labor over
     a sawhorse upon my bed she would be born
She was the most beautiful baby I had ever seen
Even her little brother thought so
He pointed to each perfect part of his baby sister

Then pointed to each of his own
Ariel could not believe this perfect baby
Had just come out of mommy's belly
With its eyes, ears, and nose perfectly grown
For one year I nursed her, sang to her, and held her to
        my breast
Dressed her, bathed her, and all the rest
of the little things moms do for the babies they love
Kyrieh was sweet, my joy, a gift to us from above
Who would believe two months later I would lose my
        mind
And try to run from her and her brother
The lights of my life
I can not believe it still, and I regret to say it happened
I tried to escape through death with a gun
But somehow by God's grace I remained
To be a part of her life and her brother's
Though I would never be the same
After four months in the hospital I came back home
Glad to be with her but still depressed inside
If it were not for my two little ones I think I would
        have died
But the beauty and light in their faces made me want
        to go on
To fight my demons and embrace my shadow side
To journey from darkness to Light
At Christmas dad took us all to Disney World with
        our nanny Denise
My thoughts and feelings started to grow BRIGHT
We all had a wonderful time

Though having to be pushed around in a wheelchair
    instead of walking
Was like making one long hard climb
By spring I was manic
Dad didn't know what to do and in a panic
He finally decided to send me to Carrier Clinic
Where though I felt ecstatic and high I let them carry
    me for a time
Observed and diagnosed by nurses and doctors to be
    mentally ill
I just believed I was One with God
I never dreamed I'd try to kill myself again
I found the medicine was something my body needed
When she was two years old I'd choose to leave her
    again while on a manic high
My judgment was poor when I left my husband, son,
    and baby daughter too
One thoughtless day I walked out the door
Then married another man I barely knew
Ariel was four but Kyrieh was only two
My little bunny with the curly brown hair and
    beautiful brown eyes
But I was smart enough to leave her in the tender
    loving care of her dad
And came to visit often after a bit of time
Upon coming home from my honeymoon I was down
    in the dumps again
When I realized what I'd done
It was a blow nothing could soften
I spent three and a half months in the hospital

Trying to figure out what was wrong
Besides needing meds I came to think
It was with my family I belong
But it was too late
I'd already sealed my fate
Married to an angry young man I didn't love
I wanted so much to be with my bear
And Kyrieh, my sweet bunny, my precious dove
But fate would have it we would never live together
     again
And I would miss them so much
I gave them up for their highest good
For with their father I would know
They'd have a stable, comfortable life
And I'd always stay in touch
While I tried to make a life of my own with Krista
Kyrieh's new little sister
I wonder if she knows just how much I missed her
Each night when I'd go to bed
When it would be time to tuck her in and sing a
     lullabye
I tried not to think about it too much
For if I did it made me cry
Many years have passed
She is a teenager now
A young lady approaching womanhood
Nearly as tall as me
Years have passed and I don't know how
I could have ever left my precious little girl with the
     brown curls

She sings like an angel
A long legged beauty as smart as can be
Graduated last year with honors from school
She is pretty, popular and funny you see
All her friends think she is cool
When we get together now we laugh, dance and sing
More like sisters than mother and child
We love to prance, jump and swing
Our times together fun and wild
She and her siblings laugh and make fun of me
The way I dance, the way I sing
The way I do a lot of things
But I don't take it to heart
I just smile and laugh with them
More than anything I'm so thankful we are not apart
So my darling just want you to know
I have loved you always and forever
And will continue to do so
Eternally

Mom

Memories of George (April 2000)

A kinder more sensitive man I know not
When Goddess handed out gentleness and compassion
Of those he got a lot
A loving devoted father is he

A caring friend he is to me
He made me realize I can be precious and cared for by
    a man
Without having to give my body away
Though we've been intimate
Without true love he could not stay
I love and appreciate him with all my heart
Though he chose another
And now we are apart
My love for him is unconditional and complete
Like the Lord's
For my true love he need not compete
I only want his highest and best good
Even if it means our paths will not cross again
Though I think they should
Lord may he have the happiest of birthdays
And delight in your sweet Presence and Guidance
The whole year through
He's one of the sweetest men I've ever known
And Lord knows I've known a few

Happy Birthday Precious Friend
Love, Meryl

Today is the First Day of the Rest of My Life (May 2000)

Today is the first day of the rest of my precious life!

I am newly born in each holy moment
as I continually open to the grace and love of the
      Magnificent One
I choose to think only high positive thoughts of my
      beautiful Self
And all others in my world
I am authentic and allow my feelings to flow
I am one of the most courageous and beautiful Beings
      of Light
in the Whole universe
This entire cosmos is a manifestation of My Light
It is the grace of God and my guides who have
      brought me
to the eternal awareness of Who I truly Am
I love myself completely and unconditionally
Now and forever.

Rev. Meryl Niranjani

They Kept Her in the Closet (Nov 2000)

They kept her in the closet
Away from family and friends
With their secret dirty laundry
Not willing to make amends
For years of lies and ostracism
They could not look her in the face
Afraid to look at past misdeeds

They must keep her in her place
Locked away in the closet
Away from friends and family
At Christmas it hurt especially
To be the only one not invited
To sit around the family tree
She's never met her nephews and nieces
Nor her stepbrother's wife
Shunned from weddings, christenings, and holidays
    She makes herself a quiet life away from them
Alone with her youngest child
Though mom is always near
When her two eldest are taken away after Christmas
    brunch to visit the other side
    She can't help but shed a tear
    What should be a day of celebration
    A day of unity and giving
Is a sad one that has her question at times
What's the use of living
Don't they know the pain they're causing
While they make merry and smile
Their eldest child is suffering
Lonely and crying in the closet all the while
They are shaking hands, kissing, and hugging
Pretending everything's just fine
One Christmas she spent all day on the couch alone
While they wined and dined
She was the victim but she's the one who's punished
Sentenced to a life of damnation
A life of separation

In the closet
Alone   with the family's dirty laundry
If only they had the courage to talk
They could set everyone free
Don't they know from the truth they can not flee?
For all their pretense at being happy
Guilt shows up as alcoholism, dementia, and disease
Don't they know she forgave a long time ago for past
    misdeeds
But being forgotten in the closet is way too much to
    bear
Sometimes she wonders will they ever care
She is a butterfly and must be set free
To fly, love, and bless all with her beauty
They've kept her in the closet for over a decade now
They have already missed so much
The birth of another sweet grandchild
As well as her first ten years
What a shame they have not been in touch
Because of foolish fears
She wonders if he really wants to go to his grave
Without ever seeing her again
Without having made amends
All she wants is a chance to talk and share
A chance for them to be in relationship
Will they ever open the closet door
and set the Woman child free
Only God knows. What will be will be
I know it's my choice alone to empower me

Meryl

Cacophonous Journeys (March 2001)

Squawking squadrons of garrulous geese
Soaring south toward winter warmth
Flying free geometrically

Scores of squealing pigs
Herded headed for slaughter
Fattened friends find freedom in death alone

Early Morning Heaven (March 2001)

for G.G.

I awake to your smooth body beside me
The sun is not yet risen
I don't know what time it is and I don't care
I'm just content to be near you
So happy to know you're there
Beside me where I can snuggle my butt into your bare
      warmth
Listen to you breathe
I feel you stir a little
Not wanting to go back to sleep yet
I stroke your arm and chest softly

Pressing my breasts, belly, and pelvis into you even
closer
We find each others' lips and you stroke my face
Lying in your arms is the most heavenly place
You begin to explore all my soft round curves right
down to my knees
When you cup my breasts and stroke my nipples you
know just how to please
You make me gasp from the sweet sensation
My passion grows as my inner lips get moist
As you caress my smooth round bottom I feel the
pleasure grow
And I shudder as you pull me into your pelvis and
warm expanded penis
Which I have softly caressed and pulled to its full
extent into my warm belly
I enjoy feeling the delicate folds of the sacs around
your balls
I softly massage, lick, and kiss them
Slowly I run my tongue over the shaft of your penis
And as I suck we are both in bliss
You explore the soft wetness of my pussy which
makes me want to have
All of you deep inside me
So you help me climb on top and ride you rocking for
a while
Feeling the pleasure, the closeness, the caring
Makes my beautiful body and soul sing and smile
You kiss me deeply and our tongues dance

While I squeeze my inner muscles around your
    throbbing manhood
It makes me feel ready for romance
But we are both tired as it is way before daybreak
So we let the passion subside
It is enough just to be connected
To let you linger inside me for some sweet moments
    of kissing and quiet embrace
You spoon me from behind with one arm resting on
    my breast
And the other under me holding me close to your bare
    furry chest
While we snuggle and fall back to sleep until the day
    breaks and the ringing phone wakes
Us to begin another glorious day in a Jamaican
    paradise

Good intentions Backfired (2001)

I tried to do a good deed
To be kind to one I believed to be in need
At first I wanted to help a friend and bring a smile
To a man in prison who had not had one for a while
Things went awry
Needs and desires got out of hand
We caused my friend, his beloved to cry
I found it hard to take a stand for truth and loyalty
For what I thought was right

And now I feel misunderstood
Used and abused, but if I could I would
Set things right
May we all be friends
Brother and sisters are we
May we be of one heart and mind
To experience divine Unity

Meryl

I Miss my Friend Janet (June 2001)

As I sit here gazing at the summer's dawn in wonder
     and delight
I wonder what has become of my precious Friend
     Janet
The best friend and Sister I thought I knew so well
the One who helped me bring my precious baby Kyrieh
     into the world
the One who held my hand and made me laugh at Life
     when it got rough
the One with whom I used to dance with joy around
     the living room, in co-ops and in shopping malls
I am short and she is tall
Where has my Precious Angel Nymph gone?
Father, it seems she has become lost in fear and
     jealousy

Judgment of others who are just like Herself
She has somehow fooled herself into believing she
    knows better for another
what Her Life Path will be

It appears ego has overtaken her Heart and sense of
    Divine Clarity
Somehow her mind has gotten the better of her
For she has again deeply hurt a Sister who loves her
    dearly
Unconditional Love & Acceptance of Self and Others
    is the only way to True Freedom
And Bliss, my Precious Friend Janet
So I must accept your need to be separate from me
    and love you though I miss you a lot
I will hold the space for our Union until you have
    restored your Self to the Mountaintop
Know you are always in my heart and mind as I think
    of you in the Highest Light that You Are

Meryl Niranjani

Moving On to Our Greater Good (May 2001)

For Doug

I guess the timing was not right for us

Winter cold and darkness was not conducive to
     having fun
Camping trips, canoeing, or getting thrown
Into the White River was simply out of the question
You felt sick and tired
Hurt and angry about Sue
Not ready for real relationship
There was not much I could do but give to you
And love your wounds exactly as you were
I wished to care for you and help you heal all the pain
     inside
I gave everything I had expecting little in return
But so much giving without being loved back would
     soon leave me drained I'd learn
I wanted to serve you at first and for your gentle
     company I'd yearn
But then I found out I wanted more
When I began to have expectations you began to shut
     the door
Now I'm picking up the pieces of a broken heart and it
     is hard
There was still so much love, joy, and fun I wanted to
     share
And it hurts to know you simply don't care
Yet with your leaving I've found God is still there
My Divine Friend comforts me and says let it go
I will take care of your every need
Trust me, have faith, pick up the garden hoe
And tend to the weeds of doubt and anxiety in your
     mind

"Give it all to Me", He says.

You have sight, but you are acting blind

You've been like a tiny bird fighting for a few crumbs
of bread

When you are an Eagle and my Kingdom is yours for
the asking

Go inside your heart and get out of your head

What I have planned for you is so much greater than
you can imagine

Beyond your wildest dreams, my child

So send your beloved Brother off to his new friends
and adventures with a blessing

The love you search for is within

Become still and feel your heart's joy.

It has not left you

It's what connects the two of you to Me and every girl
and boy

So I thank you, dear, for all the gifts you gave and the
lessons I've learned

Thanks for setting me free to find my greatest Good

I wish you so much peace, love and joy.

I've Done It Again (November 2001)

I've done it again

Become involved with a man who cares for another

How does it happen over and over?

What payoff can I possibly get?

There's no lasting love or friendship
Another man just passing through
Lord, how do I stop this pattern
What do I do to lift myself up and out of this painful
    drama
Let go of old guilt and trauma
How do I stop feeling unworthy and impure
Please help me to stop caring for others needs before
    my own.
When will I honor the dignity and purity of
Sweet priestess Niranjani
And allow one special helpmate and friend
A true spiritual partner enter my life
Taking time to know and embrace the "REAL" me
Oh Lord, heal this sweet wounded child
Who desperately wants to become a complete woman
And the Goddess she is meant to be
Lord, please help me surrender my old ways and be free

Meryl Niranjani

Diamond in the Rough (July 2002)

I'm a diamond in the rough
Make me sparkle, make me tough
Tough enough to shine my light
Through the darkness of the night
Spreading truth and sending love

To all God's children here and above
In heaven and on earth we stand
Waiting to take His gentle hand
Waiting to hear His holy command
How long can God's love be denied
Just throw away your precious pride
He is your guardian and your guide
As on the waves of life you ride

Rev. Meryl Niranjani

My Beloved Husband (May 2003)

I Am your wife, your holy Niranjani, my Eternal
    Friend
I meet you in the stillness
Beyond ideas of good or bad
Wrong or right
As we revel under crumpled comforter
Intertwining loins of Light

Meryl Niranjani

For My Divine Friends (April 2004)

Oh my beloved friends, guides, and Teachers

How can I thank you for this blessed new day
For my precious Life, my love
the Sunshine in my Heart and in my smile
My own glorious Self in all its beautiful
     manifestations
I Am Yours
You are Mine
My cup runneth over with joy, love, and gratitude
I am finally learning to love my Self
All of self
the "good", the "bad", and the "ugly"
Even the ugly is not abhorrent to me now
It is only a different perception
Another way of comparing and expressing
The variety of colors of my Light
I Am So Beautiful because of You
Thank you for becoming All That I Am
so that I can be All I can Be
Just to be myself is so much fun
It is pure Joy
I Am Joy itself!
What can I give in return to thank You, Dear One
You need nothing and all I have
Is this blissful, breaking, humbled heart
I bow to your precious lotus feet, Divine Friends
I offer my life to you
I finally feel worthy enough to serve in whatever
     capacity you need
I Am ready to take my place among You
Who have dedicated your lives infinitely in service

Meryl Ann Olson

To the Great I Am

Meryl Niranjani
Dedicated to Archangel Michael, Jesus, Kwan Yin,
    and Mother Mary

~/~

My Love (Aug 2004)

**written at Dukes Farm during Dodge Poetry
    Festival**

You are with me, my beloved
Here in this Circle of Life
In this yellow golden green garden of delight!
You are the One whose love overcomes me
It is for you alone that I forget Who I am and become
    a madwoman
But somehow you always remind me gently or with a
    kick in the pants
If I dally too long, fumbling blindly in the dark for
    that cord of Light that I Am
I Am your Sister, I am your Brother
I Am your wife, your holy Niranjani, my Eternal
    Friend
I will meet you in the stillness
Beyond ideas of good or bad
Wrong or right
Truly there is nothing, my sweet Lord

But our precious LOVE and Light

Heifer International (Feb 2005)

Two, Four? Eight? Twelve?
No--Twenty-Four children die each minute from
      starvation
1440 children die from hunger each and every hour
Over this senseless tragedy we have the power
To bring hope
By bringing a gift of a cow, a chick, a goat
A friend and provider
To these sad moms and dads
Heifer brings the gift of love
One goat, pig, ox or cow does Heifer send
To families near and far
Who have no extra bread in their money jar
Fifty per cent make less than two bucks a day
For all their toil and trouble
This is not the way of God
For peace and justice
We must make a fair wage for all
Help Heifer International answer the call.

~/~

The Agony & The Ecstasy (Feb 2005)

for G.S.
My darling I miss you so
Life is just not as sweet without you by my side
Going to sleep with you so comforting and natural
Waking up next to you feeling your warmth and hairy
    flesh is pure joy
A promise of ecstatic morning union
What a great way to start my day
My bed without you in it feels so unkempt and empty
Sheets in disarray and I don't even care
Once I was so happy by myself
Grateful for an occasion to be intimate with a few
    friends
But knowing you has ruined my former contentment
No one else can take your place
Though the sun is shining my heart is gray knowing
    you are there
And I am here
I am no longer content to settle for my old life
I am growing into a more mature idea of union and
    special commitment
With only One who cherishes me whom I can love
    and adore
Darling it is you
You are that special man, the partner I have
    searched for
With whom I can share the blessings & challenges of
    life

Honey I am ready to surrender to All that you and
      Love has to offer
You are my One true Beloved

~/~

Compared to Losin' You (April 2005)

Honey you are there and I am here
You're with her and I'm alone now
People are talkin' bad about me, honey
Seems like someone's out to get me
I never hurt anyone and this sure isn't fun
Still I smile, sing and dance to the stereo you gave me
Still got your pictures on the wall and on the piano
      you used to play me
I wish you were here to hold my hand and tell me it
      will be OK
But you don't care about me anymore, so I live and
      love just for today

My friends wonder how I stay calm and happy despite
      my trials
I say it's nothing compared to losin' you, babe
I already died the day you left and broke my heart
Since then Goddess made me strong
I think I can survive anything
Let them talk about me
I won't waste time on worry
Sad lonely people like to gossip and think the worst

I love myself so does my Lord
In my life I put Him first
But the day you said good-bye and made me cry
Was the saddest day of my life
You know I wanted to die

I am stronger now and I still love you
I wish you'd come home to me
There's a hole in my bed where once lay my beloved
A million friends and lovers can't take your place dear
Please keep me in your prayers and think of me now
        and then
If I have to wait through eternity for you I will
For you are my Forever friend

Chorus

I wish you were here to hold my hand and tell me it
        will be OK
But you don't care about me anymore, so I live and
        love just for today

Rev. Meryl Niranjani

All the Parts of Me (May 2005)

So much has happened since you broke my heart
I don't even know where to start

You were so mean to me, honey, that at first I went
    into shock
Even you admit I did not deserve to be hurt like that
You gave me so many mixed signals
Beautiful week-ends together and cards declaring
    your everlasting love
Only to pull away by the next and retreat into your
    own space
I never believed I would get over you
Just didn't believe life was worth living
Never thought I'd be open to loving or giving my
    heart to anyone again
As far as I could see my life was over, my heart and
    soul closed for good
Never believed I'd be happy again, never thought I
    would
Until I asked the Lord to heal my heart and He
    reminded me Who I was
That He was within and all around me
He said to trust he'd bring me a better man
When I stopped resisting His Plan
Then He began to put all the broken parts of me back
    together
Pieces of me that were hidden, dormant, black, and
    ugly
Parts where there was sadness, shame, and fear
Since daddy first touched me and left me and mom
    for her best friend
I've never been whole, just been running from one
    man to the next like a gypsy wild and free

Couldn't trust just one good man to love and
    cherish me
A higher part of me knows I'm not a victim
That you can't hurt me unless I agree
But did you never once stop to think of what would
    become of this gentle woman
Who loved you so much while you were cheating and
    telling lies
Did you ever once think of me?
All the times you pulled away and the times you'd
    criticize the way I sang or the way I think
You laughed at my hopes, plans and dreams
Your words could cut me to the quick like a knife in
    my heart
I'd make excuses for you 'cause I never wanted us to
    part
But now I'm strong enough to live without you
Strong enough to see you never were the perfect one
    for me
I've stopped crying and I can see the future in my
    mind
You and she won't last for women come and go
Even you said you did not know where you two would
    be a year from now
I'm sure she'll never love you or make love to you like
    me but I don't care anymore
You just don't deserve me
There's another prince waiting in the wings
Already knocking at my door

Who wants to love and cherish me in his own
    sweet way
And I know when you come to your senses you'll be
    sorry one day

Meryl Niranjani

The Story of Our Love (June 2005)

When I was led to you two years ago I knew you were
    "the One" for me because you told me so
The first time we kissed I had my hand on your heart
    and a roomful of people disappeared
Felt so right thought we'd always be together
Even in rough times you said we'd always work things
    through
Now it's time for us to part for there is someone new
    in your home and in your heart
At Christmas your card said you would always
    love me
Thanking me for my tenderness and two wonderful
    years together
Said I was a beacon of Light in your life
But you'd already met your new love in the fall
And that's when into an endless pit I started to fall
We spent a passionate early Valentine week-end
    loving and bathing together in the sleazy hotel

jacuzzi watching porn after a romantic dinner
for two
'Twas was not my thing but I did it just for you

But the next weekend you said you wanted your space
Oh how I wanted to drive up to Mass to be in your
arms if only for one day at your place
I was so hurt and angry I vowed I'd never drive up to
you again
The next week-end your car needed work
By the time you finally came down on the Ides of
March I felt sick and depressed
I felt shut down when you wanted to touch me and
knew I was starting to go berserk
You had changed, I knew you wanted me no more
Never again would I see your handsome face at my
door
It was nearly the end of March before you finally got
up the courage to tell me the truth about "her"
I just wanted to die, so I went into shock
For weeks all I could do was cry
Woke up thinking about you each night and space out
in front of the TV
I wanted to kick and scream, rage and fight against all
the pain
Make you come back to me, make you love me again
It's been so tough letting you go but I want you to
know
I'm back in love with me again
Wild and free again

I still feel you on the inside
Ours was no ordinary love
I still get a warm glow in my heart when I think
    of you
A pulsing in my heart and soul when I make love to
    myself
I recall the ecstasy in your eyes as they gazed back
    at my beautiful reflection as we sat across from
    each other On the couch loins intertwined
Our hearts and souls dancing together
You licking my sensitive feet and sucking my pretty
    red painted toes
I imagine your handsome face as you'd breeze
    through my door on a Friday night after a long
    week at work and even longer journey on the
    road to Jersey
The traveling must have been a heavy load but you
    rarely complained until the end
The tears I have shed over you have washed me clean
    and I am born anew
Ready to be and do and have whatever and whomever
    I want at the perfect time
I love myself with a renewed passion and fervor like I
    have not known
I Am ready to embrace my power again
To be all that I can be just for me, for Goddess, and
    humanity
My mind fully alive and awake, but becoming still
I have claimed me for my very own

Our love, dear one, is still inside me and lives on
     forever in our One Heart

$$\sim/\sim$$

The Love I Miss #2 (July 2005)

for G.S.

I miss the ecstasy reflected back at me from burning
     brown eyes into mine
When I'd sit on your lap across from you on your
     couch or mine
The bliss we felt complete and divine
How could you give all that up to check out
     someone new?
When you knew how it would crush this
     tenderhearted soul
In March you came clean and asked if I'd want to get
     together one last time
God NO I felt so hurt, betrayed, I couldn't breathe
You said you hoped Krista & I were not mad
And that you hoped I'd find another man with whom
     to cuddle
You jerk-off how could I move on so quickly or even
     be angry when I felt so attached!
I loved you with all my heart
I devastated, went into shock, became numb
You were the only man I ever loved with all my heart
     and soul in a very long time
How could I ever think of loving another

Only weeks after you'd professed your eternal love
    for me
In April you knew I was a basket case yet you chose
    to stay away
Slammed for good the door to your heart that once
    you shared but why
Almost drove to your doorstep one thoughtless day to
    take an overdose and die
To make you notice me
To force you to stop ignoring my pain
Just to make you cry, to make you show me you cared
    again
Your lack of compassion almost killed me
But I am stronger and wiser now
I see you as a cold, selfish man as opposed to a god
Whose dick is not only hard and stupid but also blind
You've yet to give me a sincere apology for the pain
    you caused my innocent child and me
You were a fool and you lost the best woman you'll
    ever have
Sometimes wish we could go back and celebrate the
    love and joy we once shared
But we'll never cross paths as lovers or friends again
I've become a free spirit gypsy with no ties, promised
    to God alone
Hard to believe I'm a one-man woman wanting a
    Sunday kind of love
I'll try to forget our good times until the right man
    comes along
Who dares to claim me for his own

Who wants to adore and serve me the way I deserve
You have so many issues, too many walls to break
    through
You'll run from one sweet lady to the next until
    you see
That wherever you go you can't disguise your pain
You can't hide from yourself or from me
There's nowhere to go except your own precious heart
Though we travel near and far from one person to the
    next
Nothing can keep us apart from That Love
No matter what the ego and mind thinks
Is a drop ever separate from the Ocean of God's love?
Even when a ship sinks
You were a fool to turn down my love if only for
    a day
We may never pass this way again
So I will live just for today

All Things Pass But Love Never Dies (Sept 2005)

for Lucia Vere

Four years have passed since the towers fell and all
    those angels died
Today is the saddest day of my life because my
    precious Grammy left this earth plane
To go to heaven, and oh, how I have cried

I can't blame you, Gram, I guess it was your time
Don't know why but I never thought you'd die
You had so much love and Light
I thought you would live forever
Just took for granted I could always see your shiny,
	smiling face
I thought I could always visit you at Buckingham
	Place
I believed you'd live to be at least one hundred
I can't believe now I'll never hold you in my arms again
I just can't believe we'll never share a delicious meal
	with family and friends
I can't accept you won't be with us this Thanksgiving
	and Christmas
It just doesn't seem real
God, I can't believe how sad I feel
I know you are with Jesus
But I still want you here with me
Oh, if it could just be
If only I could have just one more time to hold you,
	kiss you, rub your precious feet
And tell you how much I love you
How you have changed my life for the best like no
	other person in the whole world
Your kind, gentle nature is etched on my mind for all
	time and in my heart
I know, sweet Gram, that we will truly never part
I'll not say good-bye for I know you are near
I'll live my life by your motto, "Just think happy
	thoughts"

I'll be light like you and won't shed another tear

Meryl Annie 9/11/05

~/~

Sometimes (Oct 2005)

Sometimes I still think of you
And long for what we had
I remember the ecstasy we shared
How I loved to bury my face in your hairy chest
And place kisses on your face and neck
I remember your brown piercing eyes that burned
    with fire
As I laid atop you heart to heart with you inside
Now we are apart and it is unwise for me to lose
    myself
In memories of what once was for you have found
Someone new to love
So I'm moving on
It feels like a curse that I still think of you
Now that I've seen you again with her
You are not the same handsome man as once you had
    been
Maybe it was all just a dream
A kind of illusion
I'm starting to see you as you truly are
A beautiful reflection of me but with human flaws

And I know there's another prince waiting in the
    wings
When I stop resisting God's plan
With His grace I will let you go
I must. I know I can

Meryl Ann Olson

~/~

Dancin' Fool (Oct 2005)

I'm just an ordinary ecstatic dancer
Reaching Stretching toward the Light
Jumping skipping, prancing, falling
To the depths of a self imposed nadir
Finally tired of punishing this innocent I let go and
    let God
Then my sweet angels lift me up ever so gently
So many times my love and bliss was so great that I
    got on my knees
Kissed the ground and raised my graceful arms
    toward the heavens in highest praise and
    gratitude for All that Is, All That I Am
Only to come down crashing again into dark caverns
    of not knowing
When my Beloved leaves me for another
On my knees again I put my hand on my heart and
    cry to my Lord to heal this broken woman

I pray for guidance, strength, and a new thought that
    gives me hope that I'll be OK
A devoted mother cooks for me and cares for me like
    no other with the tenderness of a child
Until I am myself again as if by magic and ready to
    embrace the mystery of a brand new day
Singing, dancing, Prancing with arms flailing
Hips wild with primal abandon
Ecstatic Spirit that is I unafraid to look like the fool
    even though I know that
I Am the One I have searched for all my precious life

What is This Love? (Nov 2005)

Oh Lord what is this love
That brings me to tears of joy
And gratitude when I gaze up at the sunset
Hold a soft kitten to my cheek
Or brush a fragrant rose against my eyes

Oh Lord what is this love that both
Tears me apart inside and mends
The caches of old hurts at the same time
That has been stored there
For what seems like an eternity

What is this love that makes me
Dance wildly like a madwoman

And sing your praises at the top of my lungs
Forgetting sleep and food
Forgive my voice for not being
Sweet and melodious
It does not do justice
To the Object of my worship
No matter my lack of vocal talent
You know my heart is true
Breaking open in sweet humility
I lay myself at your feet my sweet Husband
My beloved said I was not his soul mate
And yet my heart was not shattered
My mind remained strangely serene
I give my love and my life to you
Preparation for service to You, Dear
Has been long in coming
Yet the yearning has been sweet
Now I am ready for the final immolation
Make me your own pure instrument
My only desire to do Your will

Meryl Niranjani

Some Friends (May 2006)

for Zara Rose and Gene
There are some friends
You don't get to see often

But you still hold them in your heart
No matter where they are or how busy life gets
You are never far apart
They are true for they have seen you at your worst
But they held your hand and still believed in you
When you were too weak to believe in yourself
The love they gave like the gift of spring water
On a hot day in the desert when you are dying of
    thirst
There are some friends with whom you can laugh
    or cry
Even times you wanted to die
You are my special friends
Ones I am grateful for each day
Because you are so dear to me
I want only the best for you always
Use me, my friends, if there's ever anything you need
A shoulder to cry on, a comforting word
With a hug and a positive thought we will plant a seed
Of faith, of Truth, of abundance
I'll remind you of Who you are
For in my life you shine like the brightest star

To Be Free (June 2006)

To be free
To touch
Beyond the scornful eyes of cold uniformed men

Who have no mercy or compassion
For the basic needs of a human being
To touch and be touched
To be free to feel that divine connection
To love and laugh outdoors naked on the sweet cool
    grass
or on a warm sandy beach
While the sunshine caresses our faces
To be free
To romp and make love
in the warm womb of the ocean
To be free of the shoulds and the should nots
The cacophony of the mind's endless wanderings
Is it too late for me
Not to reap what others have sewn
Or can I differentiate between 'their' ideas and
    my own
To be free
to do as thou wilt
Just so long
as one's actions won't harm another
To be free
To dance
Naked in the sun or moonlight
With reckless abandon in ecstasy
Without caring what others may think
Providing they don't lock me up in the loony bin again
To be free
To love
with our whole hearts, souls, and Mind

That is what I wish for you and me
and all humanity

Meryl A. Olson

$$\sim/\sim$$

Love Never Dies (July 2006)

for my precious friend, Jackie

'Twas three months ago today I met an angel named
    Jackie
through my new friend, DJ
I sat next to her at dinner where she captured my
    heart with her warmth and beauty
She fed me pasta and made me laugh at her stories
Taking me in like the Sister I never had
In an instant I knew we were kindred souls
Like we'd been Wiccans and fairies eons ago
On week-ends I made her house my second home
Upon arriving at Mike and Jackie's I didn't want to
    roam
Relaxing in the peaceful presence of her loving heart
with all the flower children, nudists, and gnomes
Jackie was our matriarch
The Mother Hen to all these societal misfits
All of us feel so natural and comfortable here

Where people are authentic, earthy, and real Jackie
    welcomes all with baby blue eyes so bright
They light up the sky
Kind eyes that beckon us to stay a while, relax, chat,
    and just be free
Her heart was so big seemed she wanted to take on
    the problems of the world
into her lovely, tanned bodacious bosom
All who knew her came to share secrets and lay their
    worldly cares in her sweet lap
I sensed she was tired, somewhat troubled, and in
    need of a long nap
I tried to soothe her with massages and hugs
She gratefully received my gifts of healing touch
But a massage can only do so much
Though it's hard to accept, it was my angel sister's time
    to depart from this plane for a well deserved rest
in celestial realms where the Holy Spirit will be her
    comforter
Jackie had done so much for all of us that she forgot
    about herself
Now Lord Jesus and Mother Mary have taken her
    cares away in heaven
where she rests in sublime peace
and bliss so great it is beyond our understanding
We will miss her so, it is true
It was Her divine Will to move on, so what can we do?
How can we comfort each other at this traumatic time
    of such loss
All things physical must pass, true love never dies

Jackie will live on in our hearts forever
I saw her yesterday in the colorful wings of a yellow
      and black butterfly dancing in my garden
She and I used to dance naked to Stevie Nicks and
      Fleetwood Mac
Singing with drunken bliss at the tops of our lungs
Jackie woke me this morning before dawn in the
      happy chirps of the birds outside my window
Darling Jackie, thank you for sharing your precious
      life and kindness with me and all our friends
You have touched my heart and made me a happier
      person
I feel so lucky to have known you if only for a day
Save a place for me, Mike, Ranger, Robby, Blinky,
      and DJ
plus all the rest of your friends when we get to the
      other side
You will always be our sweet "den mother"
I know you are eternal. You have not died

your beloved fairy friend,
Meryl

Valentine Friend (Feb 2010)

Would you be my Valentine, friend?

I'll be here if you've a broken heart to mend

with an ear to lend and prayers and blessings to send

You can feel relaxed whenever you're with me
You can just be yourself and feel free
To bare it all and share it all
Your joy and your sorrow
I'll be here for you today and I'll be here tomorrow

For as far as I'm concerned you are my Valentine
     Friend
And our sweet friendship is eternal
We have shared sweet memories and we have grown
Together through some special trials
And you are in my heart even across many miles

I am your Valentine friend
and I'll cherish you until the end
Would you be mine.....

Meryl

The Dance (June 2011)

Dance is a poem of love that expresses my joy, pain,
     and passion
Life is a dance of consciousness spiraling upward and
     inward

back to the Light and Love that I Am

Meryl

$\sim/\sim$

Stoned Soul (Nov 2011)

Surrying through Mercer County Park on auspicious
    11/11/11
Drunk on the love and bliss of Self
Singing with Laura Nyro at the top of my lungs
Needing No one
Loving Every One
Stoned on Grandmother Nature's autumn beauty
Grandfather's azure Sky and my Guru's love
Sunshine caresses my face
I have not a care in the Whole World
Easy and free to be Me
Enjoying the beauty within and all around me
Red and Gold trees tell me they love my appreciation
    for them, for Life
New puppy Puja prances through piles of leaves
As if they are her playmates
I am so grateful for this
My precious Life

Meryl Niranjani

Your Words Make Me Smile (March 2012)

Your words make me smile
and caress my heart
Like a soft lotus brushing against my cheek
I am also hopeful
happy in anticipation
to meet my new friend John
Another gentle, sensitive being like myself
I hope I will not disappoint
I have many gifts to share

Who Am I (May 2012)

Am I these constant thoughts in my head
Never ending never dead
No reason or rhyme
Out of space, out of time
No they are not Me

Am I all these feelings I feel
They seem much more real
Though they too are changing all the time
Sometimes happy, sometimes sad
At times fearful or crazy mad

69

Am I this body
My hair, eyes, hands, legs, and feet
Back, brain, stomach, innards, and heart
Of me these are all a part
But they too will become lifeless
Just dust when I die
So Who then Am I?

I Am the Watcher, the Witness, the One Who's aware
of my waking, dream, and deep sleep states
the Source of all my thoughts and Fates
My Eternal Friend
the One Beloved become infinite faces and forms
Millions of stars in the sky in yet to be determined
        galaxies
Billions of specks of tranquil sand on beautiful
        beaches
I Am the Eternal One become Many
Being expressed as my own Joyous Self!
I Am That Love, Love Divine
You alone are Real
You alone are Mine
Never ending, Never began
Always here, always NOW
Gentle, open, allowing All
One with Everything and nothing
I Am happy and at peace sublime
Out in space, where there is on time
Just quiet Love and Bliss

Meryl Niranjani

~/~

My Love Affects All Creation (July 2012)

When I fully love and embrace myself and all
     circumstances
I am able to love each and every person
Animals, three legged, and four, the winged ones in
     the azure skies
Soft, fluffy pussycats, barking dogs, baby bunnies,
     beetles Japanese dead on my porch
Ladybugs, butterflies monarch black and orange alight
     on my shoulder
Buzzing bees and tickling cicadas crawl up my arm
     and let me pet them
Heroic horses honor me with their divine loving
     service
Every colorful flowering shrub
Purple pansies and pink petunias in my precious
     garden of delight
Red and orange impatiens, orange and pink hibiscus
     flowers trumpet the glory of Goddess
Every brilliant green bush, plant, and willow tree is a
     flowing, graceful expression of Me
Each blade of grass and the fresh morning dew
     dancing upon each one
Is a beautiful aspect of myself

Meryl Ann Olson

The dazzling brilliant golden Great Central Sun
Radiant and warm as it caresses my pretty face
Ever so soft, warm, and gentle
Powerful and with purpose
Like a nursing mother
Offering her round flowing engorged bosom
To her precious infant
I see myself in All
I love all with great passion as my own sweet Self
I Am connected to everyone and Everything
I am nothing
I am everything
I am but a grain of sand on the endless shore
Grateful just to Be and nothing more
I am the Joy and the Sorrow.
I am Goddess
She is Me

Rev. Meryl Niranjani

DiModigliani's Mistress (Nov 2013)

penned in Wordplay class

Rouged red cheeks, taut mouth
Wordless, mysterious
Voice and smile gone south
Auburn beauty with sad blue eyes

Sits seemingly carefree, disguised upon scarlet chair
in crinolined crimson skirt
Red lips, red mouth, upswept red hair against a bold
     red wall
So much unabashed passion
Painter professes his love for his model in his own
     creative fashion
Blood red nearly everywhere
Deep Red – Color of roses, rage, sex, and blood
Most likely his lovely mistress
with slender waste and bare fourth finger devoid of
     wedding ring

Meryl Niranjani

Love Tornado (March 2010)

Like a tornado your love blew in one hot sunny day
Knocking me off my pretty little feet
A hurricane of divine showers
Purifying and flooding any empty caverns
I usually stand tall and strong
But it was not very long
Before I lost myself in you
At first I loved the tornado
How exciting was the breeze
Moving at the speed of Light
You and I felt so right

Dancing, laughing, loving
by moonlight almost every night
Until one day you went away
Leaving pieces of this heart and mind scattered all
  over
Up, down, and all around
Just like a tornado you have destroyed whatever was
  standing above ground
But in your wake I have found the Center
That part of me that could never be torn asunder
The love that is inside and down under is invincible
I am not broken, I have found my own Self Whole
  again

Dream to the Perfect Destination (March 2014)

How often have I tried to jump off the speeding train
  of Life
While the train was still moving
Toward the perfect destination
Because fear rushed in
Setting off crazy alarms in my head
Alerting me to future dangers
That never come about
Because my dreams and angels protect me
It's time for me to stop all the anxious thoughts.
Come about, my friend

Calm your mind while sailing the River of Life
Using the Winds of "No Time"
It's time to think new thoughts, to turn your boat in a
　　　new direction and sail in peace
Speeding like a freight train at 90 miles per hour
　　　around a curve where you can't see
Can cause accidents
Creates danger and feels scary
Time to slow down, my precious angel
Lose the anxiety
Replace both the speeding train and the heavy barge
　　　fraught with endless cares with a steady sailboat
Get yourself on an even course and back to calm,
　　　smooth sailing
Remember those carefree summer days you sailed
　　　lazily
Upon your red and white catamaran upon a beautiful
　　　country lake
With the wind blowing through your long brown hair
You had not a care
Nothing to do, nowhere to be
Lie down and relax in the sweet grass
Surrender your cares and troubles to God
Despite how bad things look from your limited
　　　perspective
We are taking care of all these matters and you
　　　will see
There is a great Light at the end of the tunnel the
　　　passenger on the train cannot yet see

All is truly well, I promise thee, precious Niranjani

Merylee Niranjani

~/~

I AM (May 2014)

I AM All that is
The darkness and the Light
The seen and the sight
Lover and Beloved
Mother and child
The harsh and the mild
Up and down, high and low
and all the space in between
Inner and outer
Everything and no thing
The void beyond all forms
But in this body
All that I feel is real
I love to hear, to see
To touch and hug my love
To taste and smell
Though I know there is a deeper part
Even beyond my mind, senses, and heart
I AM that infinite Lover without beginning
Without end
When Mind is still I can just Be
And little me becomes Thee

Yet I am glad I have this heavenly body
With which to sing, dance, and chant your divine
      name
Dancing and prancing with wild abandon
To feel all that delicious love and joy that is Us

Meryl Niranjani

~/~

God is Love and Beauty (Winter 2014)

Only love in my heart
In my mind I see reflections of Him
Smiling back at me
      In the baby's eyes
      In gray or bright blue skies
      In the silent sunrise
      In the shimmering tapestry of colors in the
            spring meadow
      In the beauty of a lotus blossom
        In the rainbow facets of a feather
Woven into the tapestry of each person's life
I see God's love
I see my own love in
      My Lord's Beauty in front, behind,
and before me
Magnificent contrast
      A play of dark and light

My beloved Father Sun married to
Bright white full Goddess Moon
A blazing ball of glory lighting
the path on my way home
as His love guides me every day on my way
in sad and joyous places

I hear his voice as the trumpets of angels
In the gleeful squeals of children playing
in the snow
In the roar of a waterfall
In the morning birds' song
In the silent attic room where Ann Frank
found Him as she hid
when all around her was death, destruction
and despair.
I feel His love in a soft cotton robe and lilac flannel
pajamas.

I declare His love with my voice, whether raspy
or sweet,
As I think of His love for me I feel happy and
complete.

Gratitude to my Beloved Son at Christmas (Dec 2014)

Ariel, Pere Noel can surely tell you are a man of
    means
Hardworking, kind, caring, and smart
The kind of man I am proud to say
I brought into this world gently at home
One special day
Now you are a grown man with a beautiful, loving
    wife
I feel happy and blessed knowing you have a
    comfortable and happy life
You have always been here for me when I was sick,
    sad, or scared
When your sister or I needed groceries or help with
    paying bills
You always showed you cared
I could never thank you enough for all your kindness
    to me and our family
I just hope I can make you proud of me some day
    soon
Thank you and have a joy filled Christmas
May all your kind gifts to me and others be returned
    to you one hundredfold

Meryl Ann Olson

Ecstasy of the Dance (Jan 2015)

written after Dance Improv
Slowly I stretch, checking in with this body and soul
Tense and release muscles that have been holding onto
    judgments, stress, and emotions
Built up during a busy week
Getting reacquainted with my precious temple
Its heavy weight supported by the wooden floor
Aware of how much tightness there is in my
    shoulders, wrists, and jaw
I tense and let go while watching my diaphragm and
    lungs expand to their full capacity
Feeling so happy just to present with myself and
    aware of how it feels to live in this body
Accepting it wholeheartedly just as it is NOW
Little by little I tune in to exactly what it needs,
    moving my feet, hands, and knees onto all fours
Curling and curving my spine in a bow like like a cat
    and sitting back on my knees
Then I lay prone kissing the ground like a snake
    raising my head to the sky to look for prey
I see nothing but ceiling and am peripherally aware of
    other bodies around me
Moving to the rhythm of their own inner dance
Light drums and rattles ring softly in my ears urging
    me to Listen to their beat
Calling me to get up to my feet and explore the entire
    floor where I meet with other ecstatic dancers

~/~

Beautiful People (Jan 2015)

Everywhere I look I see
Beautiful people just like me
In the rain on our way into the restaurant
Moms helping kids out of cars
Making sure their hoods are up and hats are on
A kind mom helps her own mom get out and then
Offers to open the door for me
Once inside I acknowledge to her how beautiful is her
     family
Though it's Saturday, everyone's dressed in their
     Sunday best
Can't help but notice her young boy's glee
I smile at him; he smiles back at me
The hostess is lovely, our waitress kind and helpful
I feel happy and blessed
When I notice people doing their best
Though it is cold, rainy, or gray
I smile as they go on their way
Appreciation and a smile goes a long way
To brighten up another person's day
It always makes both the giver and receiver feel good
Even when a stranger is gloomy this I understood
Better to be quiet than complain
We can always enjoy a quiet walk in the rain

Meryl Ann Olson

For sharing our happy thoughts with others who are
    down
Will soon enough turn their frown around

True Bliss (March 2015)

Before time, you are
Before space, you are
The love of all things you are.
For you are love

You are love
and I am Love
We are One together.

$\sim/\sim$

My Beautiful Mom (May 2015)

You're so precious, Mommy Dear
I pen these words to say
I'm so glad you are here
Every single day

Your love is more precious than gold
Never think you are old
You truly never wear out
Let the wrinkles come

You've earned every one
Throw out your beauty creams
You have a Hollywood smile
Time to focus on your dreams
And be happy for a while

You've got so much life left to live
So much love inside to give
How could anyone have ever told you you're anything
     less than beautiful
How could anyone have told you you're no good
Don't listen to fools
No one knows you like me
All I see when I look at you is Beauty
Beauty inside and out
Sometimes I wanna SHOUT
out loud so you will get it, Ma!!!
You are as lovely as a movie star
A treasure and a pleasure to be around
Your love has no bounds
You made me who I am today
So each day I will pray
You know how precious you are
To me you are like a star
that keeps shining when I lose my way
You have always meant so much to me
Your love, your cooking is divine
Your funny jokes and daily chats are
What keep me wanting to wake up each day
Even when times get tough

Please don't give up now
Though I know life can at times be rough
Keep your eyes on the prize
Think happy thoughts
Your time has come
It's time to love, have faith in the Lord and have fun

~/~

You are Loved (July 2015)

Even when you are working hard and feelin' so tired
    you are loved
When your boss puts you down or you get fired, you
    are loved
When your boyfriend betrays you and husbands want
    to leave you for another
You are loved by Me within you and above for you
Even when you are down and out
Wonderin' what life is all about I will be true to you,
    beloved child
Yes, you are completely and eternally loved
Especially those times you think I've forgotten you
    when others have forsaken you
I AM there and you are loved
Even when you think no one else could ever care, you
    are loved
I love you more than you could know, I will be there
More than your grandparents, mom dad,
best friend, or your beau

I love you, my child, as my very own Self
I want only the best for thee
So remember when you are feelin' depressed or lonely
You are loved, my dearest one, by Me
Just then try to think of Me
Forget your troubles and think of Me for I love you
    now and forever

~/~

Don't Be Invisible: the "Bully Song" (Sept 2015)

Don't be invisible
I know how bad you feel
Don't be invisible
Those thoughts aren't really real
Sometimes you think that
You are ugly and fat
Well that's a lot of bunk
I see Who you are
You shine like a star
Don't listen to that punk
Don't be invisible
Get off your couch and play
Don't be invisible
Those jerks will go away
Turn the other cheek
It's not the time to be meek
Don't let that bully make you feel sad and wooly

Stand up to him right now
Tell your teacher and your mother
Or your older brother
Don't let him get away with treating you so bad
You deserve respect and love
Don't get scared and run away
Tomorrow will be a better day
if you keep your head held high
Listen to your angels above
Stand strong and ask for God's help
The right people will come to your aid
Please don't hide away and do not be afraid
Remember WHO you are
You shine like a star
The bullies won't amount to much
But you will go very far

I AM the Diva of the Holly Trees (Sept 2015)

I Am the Diva of the Holly Trees in your yard
Thanks for caring about my flock
Many of us were dying
Thirsting for sweet rain
Summer earth was dry as a rock and we yearned for
     summer showers
But you came along while singing your sweet song

Caring enough to pull off many dead leaves and
    watering us while you sprinkled your garden
    flowers
Pruned and tore off many dead branches that were
    draining our strength
Using your bare hands or a simple scissor
Though you felt incompetent it was your loving
    kindness we felt
You watered as many of us you could reach with your
    new garden hose
And came to love and appreciate our new leaves we
    wanted to produce just to show our gratitude
Even the trees you could not reach with the hose felt
    your love for the Whole
We worked hard to grow new green leaves just so you
    could appreciate our beauty
We felt much joy from your love and caring
    handiwork we felt renewed
Your beautiful songs made us feel like we belonged
    to you
We love you for the refreshing showers and many
    hours of care
You gave in the morning and hot noonday sun without
    thought of food or compensation
Now we have new berries, new leaves sprouting in
    abundance from our trunks
And we are very grateful
Listen, my Divine Friend, as a we sing our quiet tones
    of Love

and Appreciation for thee
Love from the Diva of the Holly Trees

channeled through Meryl

~/~

Magical Child (Oct 2015)

Never did I think I'd be
Alive and happy at sixty years of age
A mother, daughter, and Liam, our pride and joy
He lifted me up this summer when I was down
Liam's smile can turn any frown around
In this magical child's divine Presence I feel complete
For his love no one need compete
A love so gentle, guileless, and sweet
Who would think this tiny child
Could settle and calm me more than any drug
For I am a gypsy, free and wild
When Liam comes to stay
I don't want to run away
Just want to be still and hold him most of the day
I sing to him, we laugh, love, and play catch or hide
    and seek
When he sees me he has a smile from ear to ear
He recognizes his Grandma who holds him dear
His joyous laugh so contagious it makes my heart soar
    with glee

Meryl Ann Olson

When most strangers and visitors all want to come see
    our little Lee
I feel so blessed and grateful to have Liam in my
    precious life

Grandma Meryl

~/~

Equanimity (Nov 2015)

for Gary

I met him in our twilight years
When I was not really looking
The time when kids are grown
And usually out of the house
We seem to be opposites
I'm vociferous while he's quiet as a mouse
I like loud music while he wears ear plugs around the
    house
When he speaks his words are always wise, funny,
    true, and kind
He tells no lies and has a brilliant mind
Inexperienced in romance when first we met
While I have three kids and have kissed more men
    than Madonna and the Magdalene put together
He knows details of ancient history and sacred archaic
    languages few could ever understand
When we met I was in love with another man

One who did not really appreciate me
It took me a while to realize I was barking up the
      wrong tree
Gary said don't worry cause he loved me
      unconditionally
Though he was quiet there was something about him
      that attracted me
I could tell by his sly smile there was something
      special underneath the Clark Kent exterior
Instead of a blazing passion that burns out before
ever growing into an enduring flame
We took our time sharing with great care and respect
After some time we found an enduring mature divine
      romance
He's stayed with me for three years now though it
      seems like we've known each other forever
Seen me through twelve seasons of ups and downs, a
      lot of laughter, some craziness, and blues too
And still he chooses to hang around
He is the kindest man I've ever known
And so patient with my moods
He even sees the best in me when I get depressed or I
      want to brood
I love to watch him hold kittens, pet dogs, and cats
When he spends time with me or one of our pets his
      attention is transfixed
He's so focused it is like no one else is in the room
My precious helpmate is happy at home alone or quiet
      with his lady by his side
While I like to dance and run around

But I am starting to settle down and in him I have
found a gentle man, a true love who is sweet and
settled
In his lasting, gentle embrace I have found equipoise
Happy to be still for a change
Except when the kids and grandson come over
Gary helps me with them, and my mom too
Knowing he has my back and nothing upsets him is
such a gift
His quiet strength a rock that gives me a lift if I
need one
His loyalty and unconditional love a Godsend
He is my angel on earth
With my man at my side my dreams have been given
new birth and I am so grateful

love, Meryl Ann

Heartscapes (Nov 2015)

The heart is a vast open space
The hub of all that is sacred
Great thoughts, things and Beings
PURE CONSCIOUSNESS
A beautiful landscape of colors, textures, and feelings
A magnificent tapestry woven from threads of Light,
love, and infinite Intelligence
My Heart, How Great THOU ART!

CPSIA information can be obtained
at www.ICGtesting.com
Printed in the USA
FSHW02n1557091018
52858FS